P9-BZT-012

WITHDRAWN

Primeras damas/First Ladies

Martha Washington

por/by Sally Lee

Editora consultora/**Consulting Editor:** Gail Saunders-Smith, PhD

Consultor/Consultant: Carl Sferrazza Anthony,
Historiador de la Biblioteca Nacional de Primeras Damas en Canton, Ohio/
Historian National First Ladies' Library in Canton, Ohio

CAPSTONE PRESS
a capstone imprint

Pebble Plus is published by Capstone Press,
151 Good Counsel Drive, P.O. Box 669, Mankato, Minnesota 56002.
www.capstonepub.com

Copyright © 2011 by Capstone Press, a Capstone imprint. All rights reserved.
No part of this publication may be reproduced in whole or in part, or stored in a retrieval system, or transmitted
in any form or by any means, electronic, mechanical, photocopying, recording, or otherwise, without written
permission of the publisher. For information regarding permission, write to Capstone Press,
151 Good Counsel Drive, P.O. Box 669, Dept. R, Mankato, Minnesota 56002.

Books published by Capstone Press are manufactured with paper
containing at least 10 percent post-consumer waste.

Library of Congress Cataloging-in-Publication Data
Lee, Sally.
  [Martha Washington. Spanish & English]
  Martha Washington / by Sally Lee.
      p. cm.—(Pebble Plus bilingüe. Primeras damas Pebble Plus bilingual. First ladies)
  Includes index.
  Summary: "Simple text and photographs describe the life of Martha Washington—in both English and Spanish"—
Provided by publisher.
  ISBN 978-1-4296-6113-3 (library binding)
  1. Washington, Martha, 1731–1802—Juvenile literature. 2. Presidents' spouses—United States—Biography—Juvenile
literature. I. Title. II. Series.
  E312.19.W34L4418 2011
  973.4'1092—dc22   2010042266

Editorial Credits
Christine Peterson, editor; Strictly Spanish, translation services; Ashlee Suker, designer; Danielle Ceminsky,
      bilingual book designer; Svetlana Zhurkin, media researcher; Laura Manthe, production specialist

Photo Credits
Art Resource, N.Y./The New York Public Library, 16–17
The Bridgeman Art Library/Virginia Historical Society, Richmond, Virginia, 9
Corbis/Bettmann, 1, 12–13, 21
Getty Images/Stock Montage, cover (right); SuperStock, 18–19
The Granger Collection, New York, 6–7
Library of Congress, 10–11, 15
Line of Battle Enterprise, 5
Shutterstock/Alaettin Yildirim, 5, 7, 9, 11, 13, 15, 21 (caption plate); antoninaart, cover (left), 1, 5–6, 8–9, 20–21, 22–23,
      24 (pattern); Gemenacom, 9, 21 (frame); Mikhail Olykainen, 5 (frame)

Note to Parents and Teachers

The Primera damas/First Ladies series supports national history standards related to people
and culture. This book describes and illustrates the life of Martha Washington in both English
and Spanish. The images support early readers in understanding the text. The repetition of
words and phrases helps early readers learn new words. This book also introduces early readers
to subject-specific vocabulary words, which are defined in the Glossary section. Early readers
may need assistance to read some words and to use the Table of Contents, Glossary, Internet
Sites, and Index sections of the book.

Printed in the United States of America in North Mankato, Minnesota.
092010   005933CGS11

Table of Contents

Tabla de contenidos

Early Years

Martha Washington was known for her kindness. The future first lady was born June 2, 1731, in Virginia. Martha was the oldest of John and Frances Dandridge's eight children.

Los primeros años

Martha Washington fue conocida por su bondad. La futura primera dama nació el 2 de junio de 1731, en Virginia. Martha fue la mayor de los ocho hijos de John y Frances Dandridge.

born in Virginia/
nace en Virginia

1731

young Martha Washington/
Martha Washington
en su juventud

Martha didn't go to school. Instead she learned how to run a home. Martha's mother taught her to spin wool, cook, and sew.

Martha no fue a la escuela. Ella aprendió a dirigir un hogar. La madre de Martha le enseñó a hilar lana, cocinar y coser.

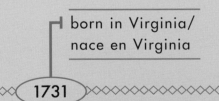

born in Virginia/
nace en Virginia

1731

Martha was born at this Virginia home./ Martha nació en esta casa de Virginia.

Family Life

In 1750 Martha married Daniel Custis. They had four children, but two died as babies. Daniel died in 1757. Martha was left alone with two small children.

Vida familiar

En 1750 Martha se casó con Daniel Custis. Ellos tuvieron cuatro hijos, pero dos murieron cuando eran bebés. Daniel murió en 1757. Martha se quedó sola con dos hijos pequeños.

born in Virginia/
nace en Virginia

1731   1750

marries Daniel Custis/
se casa con Daniel Custis

Martha's two children, John (left) and Martha (right)/Los dos hijos de Martha, John (izquierda) y Martha (derecha)

9

In 1759 Martha married George Washington.
They moved to George's Virginia plantation
called Mount Vernon. Martha was in charge
of the workers and farm goods.

En 1759 Martha se casó con George Washington.
Ellos se mudaron a la plantación de George en
Virginia, llamada Mount Vernon. Martha estaba a
cargo de los trabajadores y de los productos agrícolas.

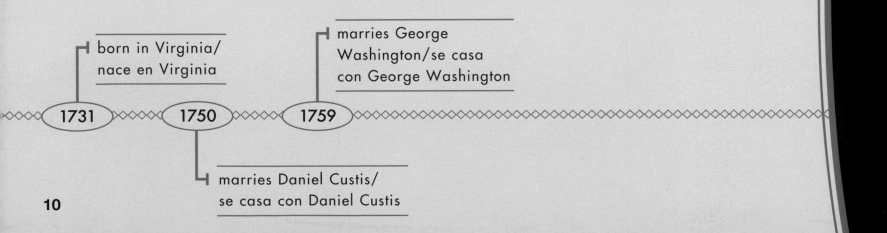

born in Virginia/
nace en Virginia

marries George
Washington/se casa
con George Washington

1731   1750   1759

marries Daniel Custis/
se casa con Daniel Custis

George and Martha Washington at their wedding, 1759/George y Martha Washington en su boda, 1759

The War

In 1775 the American colonies went to war against Great Britain. George led the American army. Martha joined him at his army camp every winter.

La guerra

En 1775 las colonias norteamericanas entraron en guerra contra Gran Bretaña. George dirigió al ejército norteamericano. Martha lo acompañaba en su campamento del ejército cada invierno.

born in Virginia/
nace en Virginia

marries George
Washington/se casa
con George Washington

1731   1750   1759   1775

marries Daniel Custis/
se casa con Daniel Custis

war with Great Britain
begins/se inicia la guerra
con Gran Bretaña

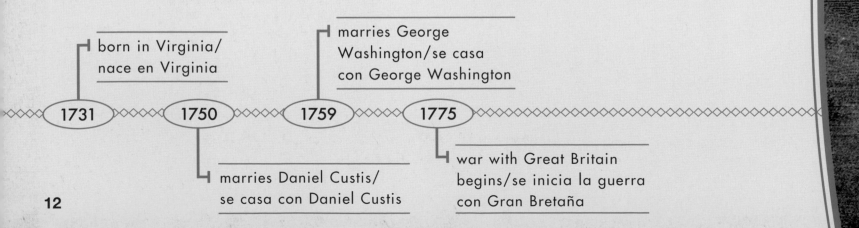

Martha (far right) visited troops during the war./Martha (extrema derecha) visitaba a las tropas durante la guerra.

Martha wanted to help the ragged soldiers. She visited the sick men. Martha knitted warm socks and made them clothes. She wrote letters to raise money for food and clothes.

Martha quería ayudar a los soldados. Ella visitaba a los hombres enfermos. Martha tejía cálidos calcetines y les hacía ropa. Ella escribía cartas para reunir dinero para comida y ropa.

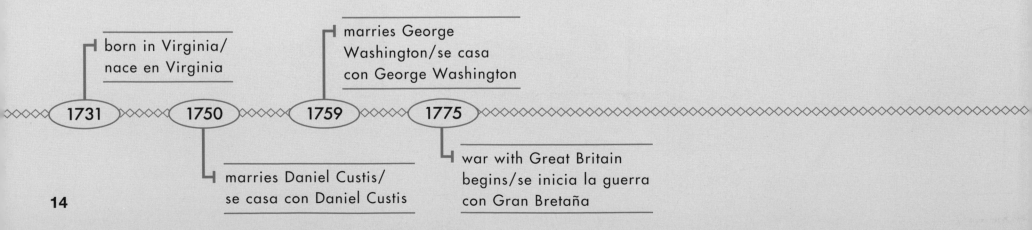

born in Virginia/
nace en Virginia

marries George
Washington/se casa
con George Washington

1731 **1750** **1759** **1775**

marries Daniel Custis/
se casa con Daniel Custis

war with Great Britain
begins/se inicia la guerra
con Gran Bretaña

Martha (center) knitted socks for soldiers./ Martha (al centro) tejía calcetines para los soldados.

15

First Lady

The colonies won the war. In 1789 George became the first U.S. president. Martha became first lady. She wanted a quiet life. But Martha knew the country needed George.

Primera dama

Las colonias ganaron la guerra. En 1789 George se convirtió en el primer presidente de EE.UU. Martha se convirtió en la primera dama. Ella quería una vida tranquila. Pero Martha sabía que el país necesitaba a George.

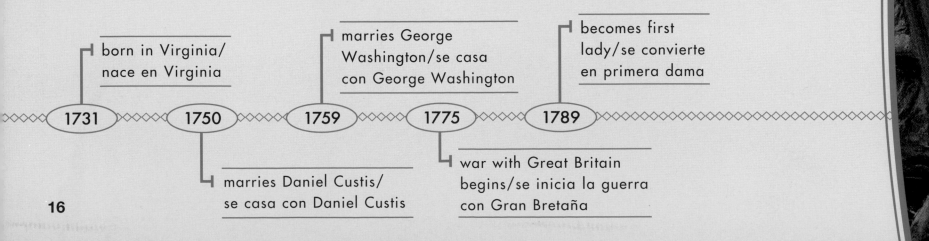

born in Virginia/
nace en Virginia

marries George
Washington/se casa
con George Washington

becomes first
lady/se convierte
en primera dama

| 1731 | 1750 | 1759 | 1775 | 1789 |

marries Daniel Custis/
se casa con Daniel Custis

war with Great Britain
begins/se inicia la guerra
con Gran Bretaña

As first lady, Martha gave dinner parties.
She held weekly teas for the public.
Her kindness made people feel welcome.
People called her Lady Washington.

Como primera dama, Martha hacía cenas.
Ella hacía reuniones de té semanales para
el público. Su amabilidad hacía que las personas
se sintieran bienvenidas. Las personas la llamaban
Lady Washington.

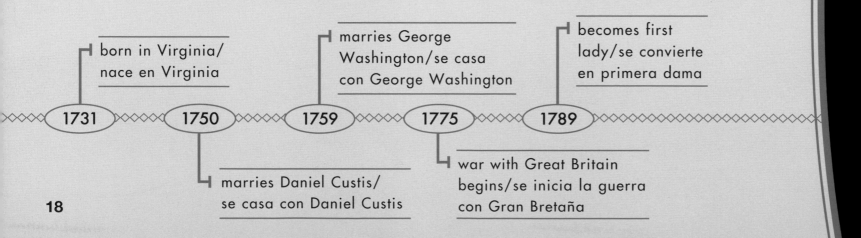

born in Virginia/
nace en Virginia

marries George
Washington/se casa
con George Washington

becomes first
lady/se convierte
en primera dama

1731   1750   1759   1775   1789

marries Daniel Custis/
se casa con Daniel Custis

war with Great Britain
begins/se inicia la guerra
con Gran Bretaña

19

George was president for eight years.
He died in 1799. Martha was too sad to
go to his funeral. In 1802 Martha died
at age 70.

George fue presidente durante ocho años.
Él murió en 1799. Martha se sentía demasiado triste
para ir a su funeral. En 1802 Martha murió a
los 70 años de edad.

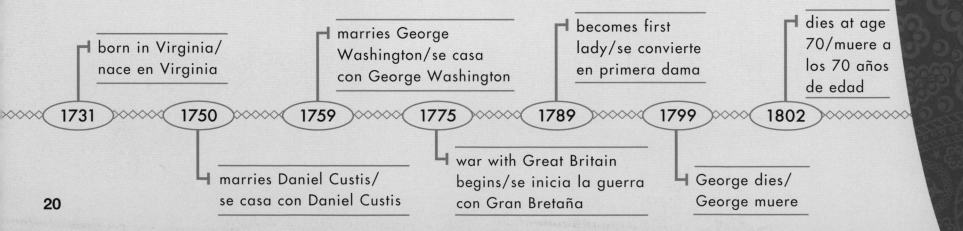

born in Virginia/
nace en Virginia

marries George
Washington/se casa
con George Washington

becomes first
lady/se convierte
en primera dama

dies at age
70/muere a
los 70 años
de edad

1731   1750   1759   1775   1789   1799   1802

marries Daniel Custis/
se casa con Daniel Custis

war with Great Britain
begins/se inicia la guerra
con Gran Bretaña

George dies/
George muere

portrait of Martha painted late in her life/retrato de Martha pintado en la madurez de su vida

21

Glossary

colony—an area settled by people from another country and ruled by that country; the 13 American colonies were controlled by Great Britain

funeral—a ceremony for a person who has died

plantation—a large farm that grows crops like coffee, tea, and cotton

spin—to make thread by twisting together thin fibers

tea—a social gathering at which tea and other foods are served

wool—the soft, thick, curly hair of sheep or goats; wool is used to make yarn and fabric

Internet Sites

FactHound offers a safe, fun way to find Internet sites related to this book. All of the sites on FactHound have been researched by our staff.

Here's all you do:

Visit *www.facthound.com*

Type in this code: 9781429661133

Super-cool stuff! Check out projects, games and lots more at **www.capstonekids.com**

Glosario

la colonia—un área colonizada por personas de otro país y gobernada por ese país; las 13 colonias norteamericanas eran controladas por Gran Bretaña

el funeral—una ceremonia para una persona que murió

hilar—hacer hilo torciendo fibras delgadas

la lana—el pelo suave, grueso y rizado de las ovejas o las cabras; la lana se usa para hacer estambre y tela

la plantación—una granja grande donde hay cultivos como café, té y algodón

la reunión de té—una reunión social en la que se sirve té y otros alimentos

Sitios de Internet

FactHound brinda una forma segura y divertida de encontrar sitios de Internet relacionados con este libro. Todos los sitios en FactHound han sido investigados por nuestro personal.

Esto es todo lo que tienes que hacer:

Visita *www.facthound.com*

Ingresa este código: 9781429661133

¡Algo súper divertido! Hay proyectos, juegos y mucho más en www.capstonekids.com

Index

Índice

P9-BYL-836

Julia Clements
ABC of Flower Arranging

Julia Clements
ABC of Flower Arranging

Quadrangle/The New York Times Book Co.

Copyright © 1976 by Julia Clements.
All rights reserved, including the right to reproduce this book
or portions thereof in any form.
For information, address:
Quadrangle/The New York Times Book Co.,
10 East 53 Street,
New York, New York 10022.

Printed in Great Britain.

Library of Congress Cataloging in Publication Data

Clements, Julia.
    ABC of flower arranging.

    1. Flower arrangement. I. Title.
SB449.C578 1976   745.92'2   76-4132
ISBN 0-8129-0635-7

Contents

Introduction

It is true that in life the wheel comes to full circle, and although after many books I feel I must have said it before, I often find myself in a gathering of different people who are just beginning to live the excitement I felt more than twenty five years ago when I first discovered the self-expressive art of arranging flowers.

It is to these newcomers to the art that I address this simplified book, for I am fully convinced that anyone can arrange flowers; and I do really mean anyone. Of course the desire must be there first, but if you are one who longs to place flowers artistically in a vase, who wishes to use colour as an expression of your character, who might wish to show friends the results of your skill at gardening, or perhaps who might wish to surprise the family with a new and stimulating flower design, then this is the book for you.

Of course later, you may wish to enter into show work where the knowledge of the technicalities of arranging flowers will stand you in good stead, but it is the start that is always so rewarding. If you have never made an arrangement before, you have only to follow the picture lessons in this book to be able to say with pride after completing a design 'I did it'.

It is the excitement of achievement which is so fulfilling, for most of us have a certain amount of creative ability within us but not all of us are lucky enough to find an outlet. We do not all have the time to take up a long study, that is why flower arranging is today appealing to tens of thousands of men and women all over the country, for once the desire is there, you can get results almost immediately. It is the easy accessibility of the basic items needed for your expression which makes the subject so appealing, for you have only to walk down the garden or in the countryside, or to go into a florist shop to find all the different forms, shapes and colours with which to make a living picture with flowers. And, unlike other arts, the results of flower arranging are ephemeral, so no matter what you create one week, it will not be there the next, and so you create another picture. It is this that makes the subject so fascinating and never ending in interest, for the pallette is inexhaustible what with the ever changing seasons and innumerable variety and colours of flowers at our disposal.

Once you have felt that you too can be an artist with flowers there will be no end to the different designs you can make. Your eyes will be opened to all kinds of possibilities and you will 'see' plant material in a different light. You will see a twisted branch and know that it will make a good outline for a few flowers placed low in a dish; you will feel the fun of discovering a chunky piece of wood that will eventually assume its place as focal interest in a design; you will, I'm sure, look, perhaps for the first time, at some tall spear-like seed heads and know right away that they will appear exactly right in the centre of a tall dry arrangement. But there is much more to it than that, for you will never again walk along a sea shore without looking for interesting shells or stones which will hide the flower holder if you are without leaves, and if you have a garden you will start to grow the exact types of flowers and plants which will help you create the colour schemes of your choice.

I have arranged this book so that it is easy for anyone to follow, whether you have a garden or not, whether you live in country or in town. But do buy yourself a pair of good flower cutters and one or two interesting flower containers and then enjoy your flowers. Start NOW and see how easy it is.

JULIA CLEMENTS

Chelsea 1976

The formal style

The formal or classical style of using masses of flowers to gain effect is typically British. Take care that your container blends happily with your room and furniture, and remember that the shape of your arrangement should suit its position in the room.

A formal, massed triangular shape is ideal for the centre of a table backed by a wall, whereas an irregularly shaped mass design, ie shorter one side than the other, is better for one end of a similar table. A classic mantel vase is most suitable for one or both ends of a mantelshelf; these are usually filled with plenty of flowers, the outsides being made visually heavier and shorter, whilst longer fine trails fall towards the centre and out over the edge of the shelf.

Formal designs call for formal vases, so avoid heavy shallow pottery dishes, so necessary for modern designs, and use instead your formal silver, glass or fine china containers, filled with the more exquisite flowers.

Flowers such as sweet peas, roses, lilies, orchids, delphiniums and the more choice flowers are considered suitable for formal flower arrangements, and colour is also relevant. Mauve, purple, pink, crimson, blue and other delicate colours are all suitable. Small choice containers filled with tiny precious flowers and leaves lend an air of formality especially when placed on antique furniture, perhaps under a lamp.

To make a formal triangular arrangement, follow the step-by-step pictures. First decide where it will finally stand, making the arrangement taller if rooms are high, shorter if low. For large, high rooms use a fairly large vase, for nothing offends the eye more than a large mass of flowers in a small vase.

For an assymetrical mass formal design (see page 24), start with the tallest stem off centre at the left, adding large leaves and flowers at the left and longer finer ones low at right.

STEP 1

Here a tall mauve opaque glass goblet is used to hold pink and white flowers. Fill the bottom part of the vase with crumpled newspaper, on it place a pin-holder, then fill up to above the rim with crumpled wire netting, bending the ends over to hold it firm. Insert six tall white iris, looking for any swerved stem which should be placed at the sides.

STEP 2

Emphasise the central line with pink tulips, opening the petals of the lower ones for greater effect. Then add some grey-green leaves to give central depth.

STEP 3 opposite

Add more pink tulips flowing forward over the rim in the front, inserting mauve and white freesias low at right. More stems of white spirea are added to emphasise fine outline. Any triangular type of arrangement can be made in this way using any flowers in season.

10

STEP 1

This formal mass triangular style arrangement can be made in any wide-topped container. Place a large pinholder in the base of the vase and press on to it a block of well soaked Oasis. If you are not a floral foam fan, then you could fill the vase with crumpled wire netting, placing an elastic band over the wire and top of container to hold it firm. Then make a triangular pattern with the tallest, thinnest flowers, the tallest stem being one and a half times higher than the height of the vase and the side stems two thirds that of the central stem.

STEP 2

Strengthen the centre of the design by adding the more rounded paeonies making sure the lower ones tilt forward. Add a few leaves.

STEP 3   opposite

Fill in from top to bottom and from the outside to the centre with shorter flowers, placing some 'in' and some 'out' to avoid a flat effect and finish with stems of the lovely pale green alchemilla mollis and trails of ivy flowing downwards to unite the flowers to the vase.

STEP 1   above left
Place a pin-holder in the base of a large compote style
container and cover it with crumpled wire netting. Tie
the netting to the vase (see page 88) and add water.
Insert three tall pale lemon gladioli with three large
leaves. I used onopordum thistle leaves.

STEP 2   above
Insert deep yellow chrysanthemums, each one cut to a
different length, down the centre.

STEP 3   left
Widen the triangular background with stems of
late-flowering white larkspur, with leaves flowing both
both forward and at the sides.

STEP 4   opposite
Place the vase on a wooden block to give it more
importance and add more larkspur for a fuller
framework, inserting yellow achillea flowing forward
low over the front of the rim. This style is suitable for
a pedestal, although the taller the pedestal the longer
trailing material, such as ivy or wild clematis, you
should add.

This type arrangement could be made using any similar plant material, ie tall and thin for the outline, rounder or more dominant material for centre, light but visually unimportant material for filling in.

STEP 1
Press a block of wet Oasis on to a pinholder and place in the top of the container. Make an irregular outline with the white campanulas inserting the first tall stem slightly off centre at the right, with the low left one swerving downwards.

STEP 2
Next add the pink paeonies after cutting each stem shorter than the other. Try to place them at different levels, not only in length but in depth, ie 'in and out'.

STEP 3   opposite
Fill in with leaves and more campanulas around the centre and add light sprays of pale green alchemilla mollis, or any other light flower such as london pride or heuchera.

16

Here is another off-centre arrangement called the assymetrical triangle made with yellow and white flowers in a turquoise blue vase.

STEP I
After placing the wet floral foam or wire netting in the vase insert the tall gladioli (one and a half times the height of the vase) with a slightly shorter one in front of it. Add a shorter stem leaning out at the left and slightly backwards, then continue a swerving line with freesias flowing downwards backed with twigs. Gladioli are stiff, so try not to use them for low swerves, they look unhappy.

STEP 2
Add yellow tulips down the centre underneath the tallest stem inserting some heavier leaves at the left.

STEP 3   opposite
Fill in always aiming the stems towards the centre at the base of the tallest stem, with narcissi and single chrysanthemums, adding more leaves or green euphorbia and ivy over the rim. Add water daily.

These roses and camellia leaves were purchased from the florist and made into a casual mass design. Recut and split rose stems and stand in deep water before arranging for some hours or over night.

STEP 1
Fill the container (a baking tin painted black) with crumpled wire netting allowing it to reach *above* the rim and insert the leaves in a casual loose triangular pattern.

STEP 2
Cover the outline pattern with roses, some tilting backwards, the bigger ones lower down.

STEP 3   opposite
Complete by adding the shorter and more widely opened roses in the centre, the low ones flowing forward. If you want some in buds and some more fully opened stand some in the light and others in the dark before arranging. Fill up with water daily.

The Hogarth curve, named after William Hogarth, the English painter (1697–1764) who, after receiving bad criticism refused to sign his paintings, but instead scribbled a long S curve and called it the line of beauty, is a line most students of flower arranging have to practice as an exercise. Many find it difficult. So here we go.

STEP 1   above left
Press a block of Oasis or any other floral foam on to a pinholder and place in the top of a tall container. Next insert any tall thin curved stems such as twigs, thin flowers or broom as in the picture, making sure the lowest stem swerves downwards, the tip being almost underneath the tip of the tallest stem.

STEP 2
Cover this outline, I used tulips and freesias, but any non stiff flowers would do. Make sure the stems on the inside of the curve are short.

STEP 3   left
Fill in without going beyond the outline with bigger flowers adding blossom or leaves around the centre to unite the stems and cover the rim.

Here is a softer version of the curve which shows the
rhythmic movement which can be obtained with stems
of wild clematis (old man's beard) tobacco flowers,
sorbus berries and veronica with wider opened asters
for the centre.

This loosely flowing autumn arrangement is pink and crimson in a pale green soapstone container.

STEP 1 above left
The off-centre outline is made with leaves and snow berries, the low right stems swerving downwards. The vase is first filled with Oasis held on a pinholder.

STEP 2 above
Some thin-stemmed pink schyzostilis are added to the outline and the centre is strengthened with three stems of sugar pink nerines, one below the other.

STEP 3 left
Crimson sedum spectabile is inserted in between the pink nerines and pale green hydrangeas are added for central bulk.

STEP 4 opposite
Daisy-like white/mauve dimorphollithicas are added as fillers, some tilting forward. White green snow berries and trailing leaves finish the effect.

This formal triangular style can be made with any season flowers provided you place the tallest and more pointed flowers on the outside.

STEP 1
After filling the vase with wet Oasis pressed on to a pinholder insert the tall stems in a triangular pattern as in the picture. Delphiniums, golden rod, sweet peas or larkspur could be used equally well so also can tall sprays of greenery.

STEP 2
Add the dominant paeonies, cutting each stem shorter than the other, the low one pointing out over the rim. Chrysanthemums roses or dahlias or any rounded flowers can be used for the centre.

STEP 3   opposite
Fill in with shorter flowers adding leaves or any light touch here and there. Give your flowers a long deep drink before arranging them and add water daily.

Some flowers appear to be expensive, but with a little imagination one or two stems can make a very effective decoration. Here I used a piece of root wood, two sprigs of ivy and one stem of lilies on a black painted wooden base. The wood was bought from the household stores, four door stoppers were screwed to the corners and the whole painted black.

STEP I
Place a pinholder in a dish of water at the left of the base and across it lay a piece of root or drift wood. (This is optional but adds interest). Then insert on the holder an upright spray of tree ivy, adding another low out at the right.

STEP 2
Remove two of the florets from the stem of the lilies, inserting first the main stem upright with bud and flower open, adding the two remaining flowers lower down with more leaves.

STEP 3   opposite
The same plant material was used in this tall container to obtain a change. First the wood was laid across the opening of the vase, next the tall ivy was inserted with the swerving stem out at the right and finally the lilies were placed. I used no holder, the stems resting against the inside of the vase. However, if you are uncertain nearly fill the vase with wet newspaper or sand, adding a pinholder on to this false platform.

28

These garden Iceberg roses help make this white and
green arrangement in a curved pattern. A dish holding
a pinholder and water was stood on the top of the
silver compote stand, the flowers and leaves being
inserted as in the Hogarth curve pattern (see page 22).

The modern style

If you live in a house or flat of contemporary design then you will probably be most interested in the modern style of flower arrangement. Although often appearing more bold and exciting than traditional styles, flower arrangements in the modern manner are, in my opinion, easier to achieve.

To make an original modern design do not be afraid to use strong or contrasting colours; neither must you fear heights, for tall designs are more modern than squat ones. The value of space must be realised, and allowed for round the principal lines of your design: be careful to resist the temptation to fill up the spaces in your arrangement because you are afraid it might appear too sparse.

An appropriate background is most important. If your walls are pale, you can place before them dark branches and bright leaves; if dark it would be better to use striking colours such as yellow, orange and scarlet.

The right container is also a matter for consideration; it should be plain and uncluttered in appearance, perhaps made of thick metal, glass or pottery. It can be shallow or tall depending upon the space to be filled.

Although flowers alone can make interesting modern designs, a contrast of form will make the pattern more eye-catching. For instance, a tall branch with short flowers grouped low down, or tall flowers with a piece of gnarled wood placed low in the design, will prove more exciting than if six flowers all of one kind are placed upright in a container.

So if you are interested in making creative modern arrangements now is the time to start looking for accessories so useful for adding a different shape or form to your design.

Collect some large stones, rough pieces of wood, old roots, dried fungus, shells, even ornaments, for all of these are valuable accessories to modern flower arrangement. Pieces of wood can be sandpapered to obtain interesting textures and other items may be rubbed smooth, polished with shoe polish, and finished in a variety of colours.

Here is a lesson on the rectangular line using one bunch of iris and another of double tulips with some twigs of forsythia or any other fine greenery.

STEP 1

Place the pinholder at left back of the oblong dish and insert three stems of forsythia, the tallest one being one and a half times the length of the dish. The low right one two thirds that of the height and the shorter one leaning out at the left slightly backwards.

STEP 2

Add the iris, the second from bottom low one at right can also be placed short at the left. Allow the stems to emerge from the centre.

STEP 3   opposite

Finally add the yellow double tulips low around the centre, yet following the line and insert leaves at the side and the back. Add water.

This is a basic teaching line but can be softened with flowing material when experience is gained.

Fix a slat of wood to the base of ivy roots so that it stands firmly in a shallow dish. Have ready large stones, moss and seasonal flowers.

STEP 4   opposite
Finally cut some of the flowers short, inserting them in front of the root, the stems reaching through the wood to the pinholder at back. A few leaves will make an attractive background. Fill dish with water.

STEP 3
Impale flowers on the holder – I used yellow doronicums – placing some upright, some forward and others flowing out at right.

STEP 2
Place roots upright, and hold the slat down firmly with stones. Cover with moss. Place pinholder at back.

To be modern in flower arranging you should aim high and leave plenty of space around the main lines of your design to allow for contrast. Here, impaled on a pinholder in a dish of water standing on a wooden base, are curved stems of pussy willow, the tallest being twice the length of the base.

Two aspidistra leaves are then inserted, one leaning backward, and the other forward.

Curl the leaves round your finger and fix with a hair clip or paper clip leaving them to soak in water for a few hours. When the clip is removed the required 'swerve' can be obtained. Add four bright red tulips low down for dominant interest.

STEP 2   opposite

Place white stones around the tin of water, which not only hide it, but give added effect, and place two more tulips leaning forward over the stones. If tulips are clustered together they not only remain upright but, if cut shorter, last a long time. Rub the wooden base over with grate polish to give an antique finish which helps to produce the modern colour scheme of red, green, black and white.

Modern containers are made in all shapes and sizes, sometimes with two openings which can to some present a problem. Yet they are a challenge to use and many variations can be obtained. Here just three daffodils, some twigs and two leaves are designed in a modern manner.

STEP I
A tall angled twig of hawthorn was inserted in the top opening (a wedge of wet Oasis will hold it firm if a pinholder is not used) followed by a shorter twig in the lower opening.

STEP 2
One fatzia japonica leaf was added in each opening, one angled to the left, the other out to the right.

STEP 3   opposite
Finally three daffodils and leaves were placed in the top opening to make this simple yet effective design. Alternatives could be three carnations, roses or any flowers in season.

This is an unusual pottery container, but the design could be equally well made in any upright vase. Modern designs demand space, so do not be afraid to aim high with your branches, leaving plenty of space in between the height and the base.

STEP 1
Insert an angular stem of leafy hawthorn on to a pinholder which rests in the base of the container. Allow it to lean out to the right.

STEP 2
Place some twisty pieces of vine or root across the opening some are bleached white, others painted black.

STEP 3   opposite
Insert some stems of colourful ranunculas or anemones. Spreading out low at the right and add some leaves to unite the stems. Fill vase with water.

Spring twigs are here used in a modern manner with three tulips and heather. The blossom burst two days after the photograph was taken and lasted ten days then turning into leaf.

STEP I
Place a pinholder in the base of the upper part of the container and insert a tall blossom twig. Adding another directly in front leaning out to the left.

STEP 2
Add stems of heather in a cross line swerving down at the left.

STEP 3   opposite
Insert three pink early double flowering tulips, each one cut shorter than the other and fill the container with water.

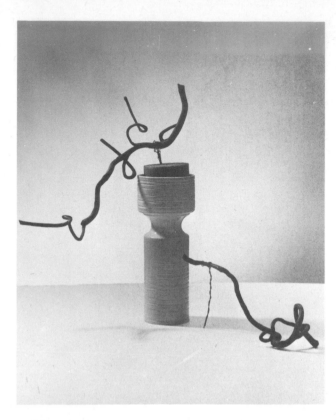

A bunch of anemones will bring colour to any room in the winter. Here is an easy way of making them appear more important.

STEP 1   above left
Place a round block of Oasis or Mosy into the top of the container and insert twists of wood which have been painted black. Give a false stem to the wood by twisting it round with wire or a thick hairpin.

STEP 2   above
Insert the stems of bulrushes for height, the wood gives width.

STEP 3   left
Tuck in short pieces of greenery to cover the Oasis.

STEP 4   opposite
Add colourful anemones and stand vase on a base and you have a modern long lasting decoration.

A shallow dish and a pinholder is all that is required for spring flowers, for they do not need deep water, just enough to cover the holder.

STEP 1   above left
Place the pinholder at the left of the dish (it could be at the right if you like) and insert a tall stem of forsythia (the height being one and a half times the length of the dish) then add another shorter stem leaning out at the right and a further shorter one low at the left.

STEP 2   above
Add a few daffodils, the low left one looking up at the others.

STEP 3   left
Next place some pieces of old tree branches to cover the holder and add a few more short daffodils behind it, with some leaves or short sprays of blossom.

Opposite
Here is the same arrangement moved to the right which is how it would look if you had started at the right. Add water daily.

46

Stripped and bleached ivy roots can make interesting
additions to many designs. Here it is used with plants
for a long lasting decoration. Ivy stripped from old
trees, should be trimmed and soaked in strong soda
water overnight. The soft bark can then be scraped off
and the roots laid in diluted household bleach for some
hours and finally rinsed. Here as on page 34 the ivy has
been fixed to a base to help it stand firm.

STEP I
Stand the ivy roots upright in a shallow dish and set a
pot of Glacier Ivy behind it allowing some trails to
wind through the wood.

STEP 2
A small pot of Maranta leaves is placed tilting forward.
If there is not much room for a pot, the plant can be
removed and placed in a plastic bag with moist soil.

STEP 3   opposite
The pots are hidden with stones and moss and a few
more roots are added low down. Watering can be done
without disturbing the arrangement.

This modern container is made of pottery, but something similar could be fashioned from a tall cylindrical tin turned upside down with a shallow tin screwed to the top, the whole being finally painted.

STEP 1
Place a pinholder into the top of the container and insert two tall twisted dry strelitzia leaves, in no matter what manner adding another low down which has already been given a false stem by twisting a thick hairpin around it.

STEP 2
Insert some stems of blue/green ruta graveolens (Jackmans blue). This lasts a long time, though any other leaves could be substituted.

STEP 3   opposite
Add two pink nerines, one upright, the lower one forward. Two chrysanthemums, roses or dahlias could be substituted.

Strelitzia leaves if left lying anywhere, under the bed for example, will gradually assume odd curves as they dry. They can be painted for modern designs and last a long time. If none are available, any tall twisty branch could be used as an alternative.

This shows a different expression of the container used on page 38.

First the two openings were filled with mauve heather, then colourful anemones were introduced in between. Finally a piece of cane was first inserted in the lower opening then wound round the back and front of the vase the end being inserted in the top opening. Cane of varying thicknesses can be obtained in many craft or art shops and should be soaked in water before use to enable you to make whatever curves you wish.

Dryads of Northgates, Leicester are the best source for obtaining cane.

Flowers for the table

The art of arranging flowers for the table depends very much on the setting and on the occasion for which the flowers are required. Suitability should be your watchword.

Ordinary everyday flowers such as marguerites, scabious or wall flowers are more suitable for the luncheon table; the more precious flowers such as roses, carnations, camellias or lilies are ideal for evening dinner tables or more formal settings.

A low central arrangement looks well if flanked each side by tall candlesticks, whereas a tall fine central design can be completed by two low groupings, one each side.

A good idea is to allow your flower arrangement to echo one of the main colours in the room – perhaps the walls, the curtains, the china or even an important picture. Or you can of course make the flowers the dominent note in the room.

If originality is your aim then *do* try something different, such as three cake stands standing on top of each other all filled with green grapes or hydrangea heads interspersed with small bunches of violets or gentians. As a conversation piece it is fun to create a 'scene' or interpret an idea. Wonderful designs can be created for tables in a modern setting with fruit, leaves and driftwood.

Your table can be dramatised with colour, so try using a one-colour flower scheme, set on a contrasting table cloth.

A particular flower arrangement set on a pink cloth can look dainty, whereas the same arrangement on a yellow cloth will have a bright gay effect; on a green cloth the atmosphere will be refreshing, but a cloth of mauve or ecru will give formality to the occasion.

Table cloths are easy to tint to any desired colour by using cold dye which can easily be removed. Or you might like to copy my idea of having a number of lengths of nylon of varying colours to place over a basic white cloth.

When planning your table arrangements the relationship of the flowers to the cloth or mats, china and glass is most important: always make your design with the entire setting in mind, and try to obtain a three-dimensional effect, ie, tall candles and low flowers, or taller flowers and low placements.

STEP 1
By using a block of Oasis saturated in water and standing in a container on a black wooden base, you have the foundation for holding low flowers firmly in place.
Insert a candle pinholder in the centre; this will give height and colour even if the candle is not lighted.

STEP 4   opposite
Finally add peach-coloured roses – splitting the stem-ends first – and tuck in large leaves around the centre to give depth and stability. Add water to Oasis daily.

STEP 2
Insert two long stems of fine foliage each end, adding shorter stems each side, back and front.

STEP 3
Insert fine flowers such as freesias following the same pattern, adding some forward centre at the front and some centre at the back to match.

This buffet table arrangement would be ideal for a sideboard or hall table at Christmas time.

STEP 1 above left
Place a block of wet Oasis on to a pinholder and stand in a dish of water at the left of a large black tray. Make a rectangular outline with tall leaves and red gladioli.

STEP 2 above
Place some grapes across the Oasis fixing them with a hairpin and add apples on sticks so that some can be raised.

STEP 3 left
Insert bright red carnations running from high at left to low at right, some pointing forward.

STEP 4 opposite
Add leaves low at left with more apples and colourful glass baubles, finishing the effect with two red candles in candlesticks. Always keep the Oasis wet by adding water daily.

STEP 1
Place a candle cup–holder (see foreground) into the candlestick, if necessary adding a piece of Plasticine for extra firmness, and set candles in place surrounded by moss or Oasis and a little wire netting. Make the outline of the design with any fine flowers or leaves.

STEP 2
Cover this outline using flowers which are a little shorter; work in from the outside.

58

Finally, add short round flowers near the centre of each
side, and use short pieces of shrubs or leaves to fill in
the gaps. Add water daily to each cup-holder.

59

A table decoration which does not take up much room, and little time to make, can be made from a few stems of chrysanthemums or daisies pressed into Oasis on a cake stand.

STEP 1   above
A small block of Oasis pressed on to an Oasis holder (see left) is stood on to a cake stand and the first flower inserted.

STEP 2   left
Continue inserting flowers all round the lower part. And stand a thick candle on top of the Oasis.

STEP 3   opposite
In between each flower on the lowest round insert a bloom above it to make a second circle, then finish by inserting short pieces of greenery. Add water to the cake stand, or alternatively the Oasis could be stood in a shallow tin of water.

60

A low arrangement is ideal for the centre of a dining table if made with all round effect.

STEP 1
Fill the silver dish with well soaked Oasis and insert fine stems to make a low triangular pattern. Each low side stem has another placed each side of it. The centre stem should not be too tall.

STEP 2
The wider opened daisy-like flowers (dimorphothicas) are concentrated in the centre front and back.

STEP 3
Pinks are added for filling in, some flowing forward and some backwards low over the rim. Pale green euphorbia polychroma, leaves and tellima are added to finalise the effect.

STEP 4 opposite
Standing on a pink cloth, flanked by green candles, the white, pink and green effect is most pleasing.

Above
This simple table arrangement is made on the principle of thin flowers for height and width with rounder flowers and leaves in the centre. Made in a shallow dish and stood on a black wooden base, the flowers are white and pink larkspur with pink roses and blue cornflowers and leaves. As this was made 'all round' it would be suitable for the centre of a table or at one end.

Left
A low fruit and flower decoration can quickly be made on a wooden tray or base, by first laying bunches of grapes and lemons on the tray, finally inserting leaves and small flowers (I used narcissi) in between the fruit in small tubes of water (see page 91). Alternatively the short flowers could be wrapped in wet cotton wool.

Pink and crimson hybrid musk roses were here held by
crumpled wire netting in a glass container to make an
effective tea table decoration to match the rose
patterned china.

A small arrangement for a hospital bedside or a side table can be made with a bunch of narcissi and a little mimosa.

STEP 1
Make a low triangular effect with the mimosa or substitute leaves inserting the stems into wet Oasis.

STEP 2
Follow the outline with the narcissi, cutting some stems shorter. The Oasis will not spill water, making it easily transportable.

Unusual containers

No keen flower arranger ever possesses enough containers to express her ideas fully. She needs so many receptacles of such different kinds that although the art of flower arrangement will open her eyes to the beauty, colour and texture of glass, pottery and metal, just as surely it will eventually lead her to the necessity for making her own containers.

Tall cocoa or biscuit tins are very effective when covered with Fablon (adhesive plastic material) or painted with a mixture of paint and sawdust. The sawdust gives a rough finish and, if finally lightly brushed over with a different coloured paint, the little rough pieces will stand out in relief. Also most household bleach or liquid soap bottles can be converted into attractive flower containers with the aid of some paint.

A fine tall container in the compote-dish style can easily be made by fixing a wooden bowl or tin to the top of a chair leg (the latter can be obtained in many household stores). The other end of the leg is then nailed to two square blocks of wood – one four inches (100 mm) square, the other three inches (76 mm) square – glued to each other. Paint with a matt paint; by rubbing this over with bronzing powder (from art suppliers) an antique or marbled effect can be achieved.

Another idea is to paint a wine glass with frosted or pearly nail varnish. Filled with dainty spring flowers, the effect is delightful. Or stand two stemmed wine or beer glasses on top of each other (foot to foot) so making a tall, dainty glass container for flowing trails of flowers.

Try binding a tin, no matter what shape, with thick string. First, paint the tin with glue, add the string, rung by rung, closely together and finally brush over the whole with *Croid* glue. *Croid* glue is the best as it dries matt and clear. Rinse the inside of the tin at the joins with clear varnish several times to make it watertight.

A mixture of black and aluminium paint will give an antique finish to many a discarded vase; and flat pieces of wood covered with Fablon make interesting bases. A potato also if sliced lengthwise and stood on a base or in a shallow dish will hold thick stemmed woody flowers or shrubs: very useful with yew and holly at Christmastime.

Many attractive containers available today in the shops seem to present problems to the flower arranger. They need not. Try to follow the basic shape of the container, ie if it is curved, then follow this curve; or if it is jug-like in appearance, think of the pouring function of a jug and make the design higher over the handle, flowing down over the spout. These are only suggestions, for there are no set rules for using particular containers. Be original if you like; I am sure you will enjoy the result.

STEP 1
Glass witch bowls or round fish bowls often present a problem, yet they can be used most effectively as flower containers, especially when filled with coloured water. Here is an idea for their use. Place a glass dish in the opening at the top to hold water and add a pinholder.

STEP 2
Impale two curved stems of orange-red *euphorbia fulgens*, or any other fine foliage, one upright and another swerving down at left, adding stems of grey-green eucalyptus lower down.

STEP 3   opposite
Next add seven gold-coloured roses, cutting each stem shorter than the last to enable them to follow the flow of the outline. Split stem-ends of roses for fixing more easily to the holder. Finally, place larger leaves near the centre to unify the stems and give stability near the centre of the design.

68

Most garden owners have netlon netting or fencing available, if not it can be obtained from household and garden stores. A cylindrical shape of it will make an interesting container.

STEP 2
Alternatively the roll of Netlon can be laid flat, with the pinholder inside. Insert a tall stem of greenery for height.

STEP 1
Cut a piece of Netlon about 12 inches high by 10 inches long (304 mm by 254 mm) and turn it into a cylinder shape by wiring it together at the back. Stand it over a pinholder in a dish of water. Insert a tall stem through the net on to the holder.

STEP 3   opposite
Fill up low down with short flowers, making sure some leaves point forward low down to hide the holder.

STEP 1

A unique flower container can be made by standing a lime-green dinner plate on top of a coffee tin, adding a smaller tin on the plate to hold tall pale yellow gladioli, a pinholder and water. A similar plate at the left can hold fruit and more flowers if necessary.

STEP 2

Insert yellow chrysanthemums allowing some to swerve out at the left over the lower plate.

STEP 3   opposite

Finally, add more flowers, some flowing backward to avoid a flat effect, and finish with a few variegated ivy leaves. An excellent design for a sideboard.

The camellia blooms, named after Camellus, a Jesuit priest, are a joy in the early part of the year. Here they are placed with some twisty branches as a background.

STEP 1
The first (left) branch is laid across the rim of the container and held firm with Plasticine or Oasis fix. The next branch has a false stem of wire wound round it, the wire being inserted down on to the pinholder in the base of the container.

STEP 2
A sprig of leaves is added downwards and upwards.

STEP 3 opposite
The two white camelias are inserted, the lower one reaching just above the centre of the rim. Water was added to the container.

74

An arrangement of fruit is an ideal decoration for a country setting.

STEP 1
Stand a stew pot on its side and fill with grapes, adding a pinholder in a small dish at the back which held vine leaves and corn tassles. Apples are held together by tooth picks to avoid them rolling about.

STEP 2
Place another tin holding water and pinholder on which large leaves are inserted at the right.

STEP 3   opposite
Complete the picture with more fruit, leaves and wheat. Place lemons against purple grapes, and light green against dark, this adds colour interest.

An easy method to build up an arrangement of lilies of the valley.

STEP 1
Place a tall glass vase inside a sugar basin type container filling them both with crumpled wire netting. In this way you can obtain three varying heights of flowers all the same length.

STEP 2
Continue to fill in with more stems, making sure the lower ones flow forward and out over the rim at the sides.

Opposite
Many people possess a copper jug which is ideal for yellow, flame and bronze flowers. After filling the top of the jug with crumpled wire netting, place the tallest flowers over the handle and allow the others to flow out over the spout. Fill in with shorter flowers and berries and add wheat for an autumn arrangement.

Above
This unusual table centrepiece would make an excellent
summer arrangement because of its cool appearance. A
pinholder was placed in the base of a shallow
green-glass fruit-dish which held short stems of lilies
with two fishermen's floats of green glass resting in
between.

Opposite
This shows three empty tin cans screwed together to
make a modern flower container. The bottom tin was
covered with Fablon, the rest was painted a matching
colour. The flowers were held on a pinholder.

81

This photograph shows a bleach bottle painted with black paint mixed with sawdust to give an uneven surface. Two black painted twigs were inserted together with one stem of spider chrysanthemums.

Tricks of the trade

Many are the stumbling blocks that seem to beset the inexperienced flower arranger, yet these are easily overcome by gradually accumulating knowledge and with a little practice.

If your beautiful mass arrangement starts to tilt forward, try pulling the whole design back into place by hanging a heavy pin-holder or a strip of lead on to the wire at the back.

If your design is well balanced, pinholders should not topple even when heavy flowers are used, but beginners can make extra sure by placing a thin ring of Plasticine round the edge of the holder, pressing this down on to the *dry* surface of the dish, and giving the holder a final twist.

Flowers will last longer when arranged if, after buying or picking, the stems are recut *under* water, then left in deep water so that the water channels become filled. Most large-surfaced leaves and leafy twigs will remain turgid and strong if left submerged in water overnight before use.

Mosy, Florapak or Oasis are ideal substances for holding stems in place when transporting an arrangement such as a gift for a friend in hospital. Soak the substance in water first, then make the arrangement; it cannot spill during transportation.

If not using floral foam, always have some water in the vase before starting the arrangement, as this prevents the stem ends becoming dry, and when your design is finished add a tablet of charcoal to the water to keep it pure.

Most flowers, except daffodils, narcissi and those which exude a sticky substance, benefit from the addition of a spoonful of sugar to the water, especially the woody stemmed varieties. Split the stem ends of woody flowers such as lilac, roses, rhododendrons, viburnum and others and remove most of the lower leaves.

If you first make certain of the exact position for your arrangement it is then easier to choose the flowers you will need. Try to select tall and fine flowers as well as shorter and bigger ones, adding leaves for depth and trails for softening the sides and front – and of course they must all suit your colour scheme.

Here are some vases and equipment. The metal cone
seen in the top lefthand corner gives added height to a
tall arrangement. Also shown are a shallow container
for modern design, a shell container, pinholders, wire
netting, stub wires, Oasis, candle-cup holder, flower
scissors and reel wire.

Cut all stems of flowers *under* water before arranging
them and allow broad leaves to remain submerged
until needed. Most leaves should be submerged in water
for some hours before being used in order to harden
them. A dessert spoonful of sugar to a basin this size
will help the leaves to retain their turgidity.

Split the ends of all woody-stemmed flowers –
preferably under water. I prefer cutting the stem-ends
to hammering them because the former gives less
opportunity for bacteria to form.

When bleached wood is difficult to insert on a pinholder, try wiring short tooth picks to the end of the stem which makes it so much easier.

With the branch firmly held in place, the arrangement can be made and finally the pinholder covered, back and front, with small pieces of driftwood.

Cane can be added to all kinds of modern containers to give an interesting effect. Try covering five pieces of tubing with glue, rolling them in grit, fixing them together with a cement based adhesive, and painting them to get an effect like this original pottery container. Allow the cane to go where it likes.

This is not meant to be an arrangement but shows the effect of a 'blob' of flowers which opposes the width obtained by the cane. The cane comes in rolls and will assume a different shape each time you place it.
Cane is available from Dryads, Northgates, Leicester.

For a large arrangement, fill a classic vase with crumpled wire netting (50 mm–2 in.) mesh, and allow it to reach well *above* the rim. Then add three cones fixed to sticks with Sellotape, to gain greater height for some flowers. These are later hidden by flowers and leaves placed in front of them.

Opposite
Use strips of clear adhesive criss-crossed over the top of clear glass vases instead of wire. This holds stems in place and is near invisible. Background: a piece of wood pressed on to a wedge of Plasticine to hold it firmly on the rim of the container.

Opposite
Heavy fruit, such as a pineapple or melon, can be held
firm by inserting three sticks into the Oasis to form a
cradle. Grapes appearing to hang from the centre are
held by a thick hairpin.

Above
This shows the pineapple in place. Small plastic picks
will hold short flowers in water, to be inserted in
between the fruit. Apples stood on a ring of Plasticine
will avoid them rolling about. A stick can also be added
to allow the apples to be inserted higher up in the
arrangement.

There are three ways of dealing with very fine stems
such as sweet peas and freesias if you find them
difficult to insert successfully on a pinholder. (i) Cover
the top of the holder with leaves or moss, inserting the
stem so that some of the moss acts as a wedge. (ii) Tie a
few stems together, inserting them three or four at a
time. (iii) If more height is needed, insert a thin stem in
the centre of a thick one, such as that of a daffodil,
tulip or iris, then impale the thick stem on the holder.
The thin stem will gain nourishment from it. This
method is often used to give more height to pansies.
A finer, more closely packed pinholder is now available
from Stanley Gibbons, *Flora*, Drury House, Russell
Street, London WC2.

A tall branch or twig on a pinholder at one end of a
shallow dish may be inclined to topple. Try placing
another holder – teeth to teeth – at the opposite end of
the branch to weigh it down. It can easily be covered
by a leaf later on.

To obtain a wider opening to a narrow necked vase,
such as is often used in churches, try inserting a funnel,
the end of which can be sealed or left open to receive
long stemmed flowers. The top can be prepared either
with wire netting or Oasis.

94